Original title:
Life: Getting Lost and Finding Meaning

Copyright © 2025 Creative Arts Management OÜ
All rights reserved.

Author: Miriam Kensington
ISBN HARDBACK: 978-1-80566-190-0
ISBN PAPERBACK: 978-1-80566-485-7

The Embrace of Unfamiliarity

I wandered into a strange café,
Where the coffee danced and tried to sway.
The muffins wore hats, quite out of style,
And the barista chuckled all the while.

I ordered a latte, extra confound,
And found it upside down, spinning round.
The sugar was salty, so I took a chance,
On a donut that laughed, inviting to dance.

Lost and Found in the Shadows

I sought my way in a feathery maze,
Where shadows whispered, setting hearts ablaze.
My compass spun like a toddler's top,
As I tripped over clouds, hoping not to flop.

A raccoon approached, with a map in hand,
It pointed to nowhere, but I found it grand.
He winked and he danced, oh what a sight,
Together we laughed at the stars so bright.

Footsteps on the Edge of Tomorrow

I skipped along, a jester in flight,
On the edge of tomorrow, all things felt right.
The future wore socks with mismatched flair,
And I waved to my past like it didn't care.

A llama appeared, strumming my fears,
Playing tunes that made grew my tears.
But laughter erupted, echoing clear,
Tomorrow's just waiting, let's give it a cheer!

Secrets of the Wandering Soul

They say the secrets are buried in dreams,
But mine are lost in whimsical streams.
I followed a fish wearing spectacles neat,
With tales of misadventure and raspberry beet.

A squirrel recited poetry upside down,
While nut collectors wore crowns in the town.
In puzzling riddles, my heart found a song,
In the chaos of wandering, it felt like home all along.

The Mirror of the Journey

I wore mismatched socks today,
A fashionista's bold display.
In a maze of random turns,
I found my way to endless burns.

A map that speaks in riddles,
With paths as clear as giant twiddles.
I tripped on dreams of yesteryear,
Now I'm lost, oh dear! Oh dear!

In Search of Kindred Spirits

I went out searching for my clan,
Found a dog who thinks he's Stan.
We laughed and played, a silly sight,
Two oddballs in the pale moonlight.

With pizza crumbs and sparkling eyes,
In this friendship, my spirit flies.
We danced like nobody's watching,
Through each stumble, always launching.

Threads of the Inexplicable

I tangled my thoughts in a ball of yarn,
Crafting chaos, oh the charm!
Like spaghetti on a dinner plate,
My mind's a dish, can't wait, can't wait.

In every twist and silly knot,
I find the joys I never sought.
With laughter echoing through the air,
The absurdity is everywhere!

Horizons Yet to Discover

With a telescope made of soda cans,
I search for alien romance plans.
The stars wink back with knowing glee,
They're laughing hard at you and me.

So many paths, I can't choose one,
My compass broke—oh what fun!
I'll take the scenic route instead,
Chasing dreams, while still in bed!

Trials of the Heart's Compass

I wandered off, down a lane,
Got tangled up in my own brain.
Maps don't work when you're on a spree,
Now I'm lost, or is it just me?

I asked a squirrel for some advice,
He blinked and offered me some rice.
Not the help I hoped to find,
But laughter tends to ease the mind.

In search of wisdom, I climbed a tree,
Greeted the birds who squawked with glee.
They chirped a tune just for my cheer,
I danced till dusk, forgot my fear.

Now I stumble home, a little late,
The stars come out, I stop and wait.
With laughter echoing in my chest,
I think I might have found the best.

Journeying into the Abyss

With a backpack full of snacky treats,
I set off on a quest, oh, isn't that neat?
I mistook a road sign for a guide,
Ended up in a cow parade, what a ride!

I asked a goat for directions near,
He just chewed grass and offered a sneer.
Not quite the sage I hoped to receive,
But his antics made me laugh and believe.

Through puddles and leaves, I wobbled on,
In a quest to find the mythical dawn.
I tripped on a root, fell with a thud,
Only to rise with a laugh and a bud.

Now I roam this wild, joyful mess,
Finding meaning in a sheep's address.
I may be lost, but that's okay,
For laughter finds you, come what may!

The Hidden Treasure of Missteps

I searched for treasure beneath my bed,
Found only dust bunnies instead.
But hey, who needs gold or a crown?
When your couch is the best seat in town?

Off I went on a treasure map,
Cracked some eggs and took a nap.
Awoke to find I'd misspelled the clue,
But ended up with pancakes—who knew?

I stumbled upon a quirky festival,
With hats made of fruit, it was quite the spectacle.
The pies were tossed; I thought it was neat,
Till a blueberry landed right on my seat!

Now with my face smeared, I stumble along,
Making a mess, but still singing my song.
Each pitfall a laugh, each trip a bright jest,
And I discover each day is a wonderful quest.

Resolute in the Uncharted Seas

Set sail in a tub, quite out of place,
With rubber ducks leading the race.
The map was upside down, what a delight,
Navigating dreams all through the night.

Seagulls squawked, gave me their best,
I handed them snacks, they joined my quest.
But right when I thought I was so wise,
I found myself lost under the fries!

I fished for gold but caught only grief,
Yet every miscast brought comedic relief.
For every wave that knocked me back,
A laugh emerged from the ocean's crack.

So here I drift with a gleaming grin,
Finding joy in each silly spin.
With ducks as my crew, we'll conquer the tide,
In uncharted waters, together we glide.

The Weaving of Forgotten Tales

In a jungle of socks, I venture each day,
Searching for matches that seem far away.
My coffee's gone cold, the toast has its say,
Yet here I am lost in a pancake buffet.

A compass in hand, it points to the fridge,
But I find myself stuck at the edge of a bridge.
With ducks quacking loudly, I start to dig,
For the treasure of snacks that the seagulls must bid.

Maps drawn in crayon, by a cat on the run,
With adventures aplenty, oh, isn't it fun?
Each step that I take feels a bit outdone,
And suddenly, I'm chasing a cheese-covered bun.

So here's to the tales we find in the mess,
Of wandering heroes sometimes in distress.
With giggles and snacks, there's a life to confess,
The map leads to laughter; so let's just digress.

From the Ashes of Disorientation

Woke up one morning with my shoe on my head,
Thought I'd found wisdom in a book by my bed.
But the pages were blank, and the cat yawned instead,
So I slipped on some toast, and off I sped.

Around every corner, a sign that confuses,
Pointing to places where no one chooses.
I laugh at my shadow, it keeps playing ruses,
While my breakfast burrito silently muses.

A hat made of cereal sits perched on my brow,
Transforming a frown into laughs, somehow.
With birds stealing breadcrumbs, I take a bow,
For the mess I've created is the best I'll allow.

From chaos and crumbs, some wisdom emerges,
In the laughter of friends and spontaneous urges.
We stumble and fumble, while the universe surges,
Finding joy in the madness, as humor converges.

A Canvas of Wanderlust

Painting my journey with colors so bright,
Each step is a splash, from morning till night.
With sneakers a-squeaking, I hop with delight,
Chasing lost marbles in a whimsical flight.

Around the wrong corner, I bump into fate,
Waving at strangers who know it's too late.
But laughter's a currency we'll gladly inflate,
Trading silly stories, each a twist of fate.

A map that's a puzzle with missing big pieces,
Leads to a garden where mayhem never ceases.
With gnomes in the flowers, the fun never decreases,
And a taco truck waits, the greatest of leases.

So here on this canvas, missteps are art,
With brush strokes of chaos that come from the heart.
Though paths may be tangled, we'll never depart,
For each laugh we share plays a vital part.

Starlit Paths of Possibility

Stumbling through twilight with stars in my eyes,
Searching for answers where moonlight complies.
The pavement's a riddle, but oh, how it flies,
As I dance with the shadows, to laughter's surprise.

I trip over dreams in the middle of streets,
Where each corner hides giggles and spontaneous feats.
With breadcrumbs of laughter as my passport, it greets,
A world full of chaos, where all my joy meets.

A lantern of sarcasm, brightening my way,
I navigate life like it's a grand play.
With my shoes tied together, oh what a display,
Yet every misstep is a role I portray.

So dust off your worries, let's twirl 'neath the stars,
In this dance of absurdity, let go of our scars.
For it's here in the madness, with giggles and bars,
That the starlit paths lead us to who we are.

The Turning of Forgotten Stones

Once I tripped on a stubborn rock,
It whispered secrets, a silly shock.
"Why are you lost?" it chuckled with glee,
"Just follow the squirrels, and forget about me!"

Around the bend where the wildflowers grow,
I found a map that led me to Joe.
He was playing chess with a curious cat,
They looked so wise, but had no clue, just sat.

I asked the cat where the wisdom lies,
With a smirk, he blinked at the sunny skies.
"Checkmate in life? You've got it all wrong,
It's the snacks and the naps that keep you strong!"

So I danced with stones and sung with the breeze,
Chasing my shadow and squeaking like cheese.
They all laughed as I wobbled and rolled,
The funniest tales, just waiting to be told.

Moments Adrift on the Sea of Time

I sailed on a boat made of used pizza crust,
The waves were ticklish, oh, what a gust!
Laughter bubbled, as seagulls flew by,
They stole my sandwich, but I didn't cry.

With a crew of pineapples, we searched for gold,
But only found jellybeans, so bright and bold.
"Eat your way to treasures, forget the quest!"
Yelled the captain, with jelly smeared on his chest.

Time tick-tocked in a game of hide and seek,
With clocks running off to savor a peek.
I lost my watch, it danced with a sunbeam,
What a hilarious fumble, a sailor's daydream!

So we drifted through giggles on waves of delight,
With jellybean treasures glimmering bright.
In each funny moment, the ocean would rhyme,
Making sense of the chaos? Ah, just kill some time!

Navigating the Quiet Storm

I stood on a bridge made of nacho cheese,
Under the rain of popcorn, with giggles and wheezes.
The clouds whispered jokes, in a misty fog,
While ducks wore bow ties, in a fancy smog.

A compass with arrows made of candy canes,
Led me to paths where laughter reigns.
"This way, this way!" the marshmallows cheered,
With every wrong turn, my sense disappeared!

In the heart of the storm, was a dance-off battle,
With squirrels on drums, and a cat on a rattle.
I slipped and I spun, but never fell down,
Just joined the parade with my silly clown crown.

When the quiet settled, and the laughter ceased,
I counted my smiles, they never decreased.
In the calm of the mess, I found joy like a norm,
Navigating through giggles, my own silent storm!

The Garden Where Sorrows Blossom

In a garden of frowns, where sadness was sown,
Grew daisies of giggles, so brightly shown.
"Why are you blue?" asked a whimsical tree,
"Let's throw a party, you can dance with me!"

The roots played the tuba, the leaves mashed the beat,
A squirrel DJ jumped, with tiny big feet.
I twirled with my worries, they laughed in delight,
As we tangoed with shadows and twinkled at night.

Roses turned red with a splash of surprise,
As they cracked the jokes that would open the skies.
"Laughter's the fertilizer, it helps us to grow,
In the garden of worries, let the humor flow!"

So we planted some joy with a sprinkle of fun,
And watered our hearts 'til the mourning was done.
In a patch of lost feelings, kindness blooms fast,
The garden of giggles, forever to last!

Veins of Daring Exploration

In a maze of thoughts, I stray,
A map folded wrong, oh what a day!
Chasing squirrels in my mind, they dart,
Is this adventure or just the start?

With socks that clash and shoes that squeak,
I trip on dreams, no path to seek.
Do I follow the signs or just my nose?
Surprise! A garden where the wild thyme grows!

A detour leads to a cake on the way,
With sprinkles and laughter, I find my play.
Lost, but joyfully, I eat my fill,
To be lost is a thrill, a cute little chill!

With each twist and turn, I learn to dance,
In chaos I find my goofy chance.
So here's to the roads that lead us astray,
A treasure map drawn in a whimsical way!

The Silence Between Directions

A compass spins; it's quite absurd,
I'm heading east, but did I just slur?
The signposts giggle, oh how they tease,
"Lost again?" they seem to wheeze.

In cafes with maps, I drink my brew,
Chatting with strangers about what's true.
Every wrong turn is a tale retold,
With laughter, we share our flops bold.

Lost in translation, I misread the route,
Yet stumble on answers I never knew about.
In the silence between, I find my tune,
As the GPS sings me a joyous croon!

Directions are jokes, really, don't you see?
The universe chuckles, setting me free.
So here's to wrong turns that grace our domain,
In silly adventures, we find our gain!

Unveiling the Art of Detours

I take the road less traveled, they say,
But it leads me to mischief; oh, hooray!
Each turn I take unfolds a surprise,
Like tripping on shoelaces or pie in the skies.

Potholes transform into splashy delight,
With every bump, I'm flying high in flight.
Soggy sandwiches evoke laughter so grand,
Detours become picnics—unplanned but planned!

Maps are mere suggestions, I think I'll ignore,
Following whims, I want to explore.
Every missed exit gets a hoot and a squeal,
In the art of the detour, I learn what is real.

So here's to the paths that twist and bend,
Where lost turns to stories that never end.
In chaotic adventures, joy will prevail,
With each funny mishap, I'm told I won't fail!

Chasing Ghosts of Purpose

In the fog of the morning, I search for my aim,
But ghosts of purpose play a silly game.
They dance in circles, then flutter away,
Yet their laughter follows, come what may.

I welcome the whispers of directions misplaced,
"Follow your heart!"—it's quite the wild chase.
Through haunted alleys and cobblestone ways,
Each ghost has a story that brightens my days.

Behind me, they giggle; ahead, I might stumble,
With a wink and a nudge, I tumble and mumble.
Do they bring wisdom or merely confound?
In the chase for the ghost, I'm hilariously bound!

So I'll don a cape and embrace the unknown,
Each detour a treasure that's sweetly my own.
Chasing those phantoms, I dance on the street,
In this funny adventure, my heart skips a beat!

Echoes of the Untraveled Path

I took a turn so quickly,
I ended up at a duck's party.
They quacked of paths untried,
While I danced all wet and hearty.

My GPS was giving sass,
It guided me to the ice cream shop.
Who knew the road to wisdom,
Was paved with sprinkles on top?

On trails where squirrels inquire,
I lost my hat and my shoes.
"Head north!" cried a chipmunk,
I followed, but now I snooze.

So here's to wandering free,
A merriment wrapped in surprise.
With each wrong street I roam,
I find new laughter and pies.

In the Garden of Uncertainty

I planted seeds of confusion,
Watered them with doubt and fear.
Now flowers of whimsy bloom,
Telling jokes to squirrels near.

Bees buzzed with a riddle,
As they sipped on nectar sweet.
"What's the secret to living?"
I shrugged, so I just danced on my feet.

The sun forgot to show up,
And clouds made shadows of glee.
In this quirky garden,
I learned to laugh at me.

With weeds of wonder sprouting,
I found joy in every crease.
So bring on the unexpected,
Here's to absurdity and peace.

A Map Made of Dreams

My map was drawn on a napkin,
With coffee stains and crumbs of toast.
It led me to the distant kitchen,
Where butter and laughter are host.

Directions scribbled in haste,
Took me straight to the wrong street.
"Turn left at the cat with a hat,"
And I ended up with a treat!

Stars pointed to the nearest cake,
I followed them through the fog.
Each slice a tale of mistakes,
With a side of golden dog.

So here's my advice to you,
Follow dreams, let them unfold.
Your map might be a doodle,
But it's where the tales are told.

Tides of the Unseen

The ocean whispered secrets,
With waves that danced and twirled.
I rode a surfboard of nonsense,
To find what the tide unfurled.

Jellyfish gave me pointers,
While crabs offered me a snack.
"Look out for a whale's opinion,"
One shouted as I'd glide back.

I dodged the fish of reason,
And rode on bubbles of cheer.
The sea's deep mystery,
Left me giggling ear to ear.

So let the currents carry you,
To shores where laughter is king.
For in the waves' wild patterns,
You'll find joy in everything.

Sunlight Through the Dense Canopy

Beneath the leaves, I trip and tumble,
My map is wrong, I start to grumble.
A squirrel laughs, it scurries past,
In this wild maze, I'll never last!

A branch pokes me, it feels like fate,
But what's the rush? Oh, it's getting late!
I chase a bee, it buzzes away,
Guess I'll just wander for another day!

The sun sneaks down, a shining tease,
I follow shadows, they dance with ease.
A pathway blooms, but do I dare?
Or just sit here, and comb my hair?

I lost my snacks; I think that's wrong,
But here's a flower, let's sing a song!
In this green maze, the joy's a blast,
Even if my compass is outclassed!

The Sound of a Thousand Paths

Hear that rustle? A squirrel's play,
Or is it me, just lost today?
With every step, the ground feels new,
As if my shoes are asking, 'Who knew?'

Each twist and turn sounds fresh and loud,
I trip on roots, dance with the crowd.
The chorus sings, both high and low,
In this wild mix, I'm part of the show!

The owl hoots like a wise old friend,
But does it know where this trail will end?
I'll flip a coin; it's time to roll,
And see if chance can find my goal!

I wave to a fox with fancy flair,
It winks at me, like it's in on a dare.
With laughter ringing through the trees,
Who needs a path when you've got some cheese?

Glimmers of Truth in the Wilderness

With every stumble, I notice a spark,
A chipmunk's chatter, the trail turns dark.
I swear it's guiding me to a scene,
Where truth hides out, like a mischievous bean!

I trip over wisdom, oh what a thrill,
Wrapped in foliage, it beckons still.
The trees gossip like friends at a bar,
While I pretend I know just where we are!

Rocks spell riddles; I can't comprehend,
But I'll dance in circles, making a blend!
These glimmers flicker like cosmic jokes,
What's right or wrong? Who even knows?

So laugh with me as we lose our way,
Chasing shadows, come join this play!
For in the wild's embrace, I find my truth,
Hidden in giggles and forgetful youth!

Amidst the Ruins of Every Day

Woke up in ruins, where did my socks go?
The coffee spills, what a lovely show!
In this messy life, I wear mismatched shoes,
But hold on tight—it's mine to cruise!

Amidst the chaos, laughter drips wide,
A door swings open, it's an awkward ride.
I chase my head, where did it land?
Oh look, it's stuck beneath a grand stand!

The crumbs of breakfast lead to a trail,
Of scattered dreams and a half-eaten grail.
Who's to say what's worth saving here,
When laughter mingles with yesterday's cheer?

From the ruins rise silly little plans,
Like building castles in swamps, with hands.
So join the mess, with smiles and winks,
In this jumbled journey, life simply thinks!

Lost in the Wilderness of Thought

I wandered off to find my socks,
Instead, I found talking rocks.
They chattered on about the rain,
And hinted I might be a bit insane.

Paved paths of logic led me astray,
With whispers of elephants in the way.
I tripped on notions, tumbling down,
Landed smack in a thought circus town.

The shadows danced like wild cabaret,
While a banana peel stole my ballet.
The only map was a joke told twice,
Each punchline lost in a world of dice.

I finally laughed till I thought I'd burst,
Turns out, the punchlines did come first.
In the wilderness where I lost my shoes,
I found joy in the nonsense I'd choose.

The Art of Getting Lost

With a compass that points to last Tuesday,
I set off on my merry way.
The only guide was my pet goldfish,
He swam in circles, oh what a wish!

I met a squirrel with a tin can hat,
He offered advice on life and chat.
His words, though nutty, felt quite profound,
As I pondered just where I was bound.

Every wrong turn was a right direction,
Found hidden gems in my own reflection.
A paper map with doodles of joy,
Showed me how to dance like a silly boy.

So when I lost my way on that quest,
I found the art of just being blessed.
The more I wandered, the more I laughed,
In the gallery of 'Who needs a path?'

Breadcrumbs of the Heart

I dropped some crumbs upon the floor,
Hoping to find my way back for more.
But birds took flight with my snack brigade,
Now I'm stuck in a breadcrumb charade.

With each little trail, I hoped for a muse,
But found instead a parade of shoes.
They danced around in ridiculous glee,
Teaching me steps to not take seriously.

A pizza slice led me to a creek,
Where frogs critiqued my sense of chic.
With laughter bubbling upon the breeze,
They flipped their tongues like acrobatic bees.

In the end, my heart found its dance,
With crumbs reimagined as a waltzing chance.
What started as loss turned into a chart,
I'd rather be lost than not feel my heart.

Beneath the Veil of Confusion

Behind the curtain, I fought with my shoes,
Only to find my left sock's blues.
A wizard of doubt brewed coffee so strong,
He chuckled and said, "You've been here too long!"

A riddle played out in ticklish tongues,
Each answer brought giggles, no need for lungs.
I had a lightbulb moment—what a scene,
The answer was simply, "You've forgotten your bean!"

With every silly twist, I made a new friend,
A jester in pants that would never end.
His jokes rang loud and confused my wits,
Yet beneath every laugh, a meaning fits.

So as I dance 'neath this veil of fun,
I've learned that confusion can lead to the sun.
In my tangled thoughts, I found a good tease,
That sometimes it's laughter that puts us at ease.

Beneath the Weight of Unanswered Questions

I walked a maze of socks and shoes,
Found a shoehorn with a pair of blues.
Asked the cat where my keys could be,
She just yawned and ignored me.

The fridge hums songs of leftover fate,
A ketchup bottle claims it's first date.
Tangled wires like a family feud,
Even the toaster looks slightly rude.

I ponder hard over cookie crumbs,
While daydreaming of life's next outcomes.
The couch whispers secrets, what a sly friend,
But all it says is, 'Please don't spend!'

With questions as heavy as my high school math,
I chuckle at the chaos in my own path.
For every answer seems too far to link,
But at least I've mastered how to overthink!

Rivers Flowing in Unseen Currents

I followed a path lined with rubber ducks,
They quacked and giggled like goofy trucks.
Navigating rivers of hidden surprise,
Chased squirrels plotting cleverly in disguise.

A paper boat sails on a puddle stream,
With a tiny captain who looks like a dream.
Raindrops dance, but my feet want to fly,
Wondering who taught pigeons to be shy.

Underneath bridges where trolls sing off-key,
I question the wisdom of counting to three.
Fish float by, laughing, like old pals of mine,
And I can't help but giggle at how they entwine.

I'll take a detour into the joyful absurd,
Dancing with shadows that never disturbed.
For in the current where my worries confide,
Lies a silly river where laughter won't hide!

The Breath of Unexpected Journeys

A left turn found me in a bakery shop,
With donuts spinning like a sugary hop.
I tripped over frosting and cake so divine,
Thought, 'Maybe I'll open my own food line.'

The map in my pocket led me astray,
To a puppet show where the puppets play.
They argued and pointed, built castles in air,
While I stood in awe; I forgot my own hair.

Airplanes zoomed past but were caught in my dreams,
A giraffe nearby said, 'Life's not what it seems!'
With every misstep, I danced and I twirled,
Collecting new stories, the best of the world.

Around every corner, a chuckle does wait,
While I muddle my way through an odd dinner date.
For the breath of unknowns, it tickles my mind,
Silly surprises make me feel so aligned!

Finding Light in the Hidden Corners

Beneath the couch, I found lost treasures,
Coins and buttons, all kinds of measures.
A sock with holes and a funny old toy,
I laughed so hard I forgot all my joy.

Dust bunnies gathered for a dance party spree,
While a lightbulb flickered, winking at me.
I asked it for wisdom; it just sighed and glowed,
A light in the mess where my worries flowed.

In closets of laughter, old memories hide,
Each outfit a story, wearing love with pride.
I can't zip the past, but I can seal a grin,
For finding the light is how we begin.

So here in these corners, I search for the gleam,
With a heart full of giggles and dreams that redeem.
For laughter brings vision to shadows once grim,
And I dance through the chaos, my spirit won't dim!

Embracing the Unscripted Story

Woke up today, went left instead,
Found a sock that'd rather wed.
The coffee pot had gone on strike,
Decided it's a day to hike.

Stumbled o'er a garden gnome,
Wondered if he'd leave his home.
He raised a finger, shushed me 'shh',
Guess this tale is quite the quash!

A butterfly beat me to the feast,
Refusing breakfast, feeling least.
With every wrong turn, I'd just grin,
Turns out the fun is where I've been.

So I'll embrace this wacky trip,
Adventure's just a quirky blip.
Forget the map and toss the phone,
In the unscripted, I am home.

The Unfolding of Unseen Directions

A signpost waved with a goofy grin,
Sent me in circles, didn't know where to begin.
Each daffodil whispered a secret so loud,
While I danced with squirrels, feeling quite proud.

Found a café that served pickled pie,
Surrounded by laughter, I couldn't deny.
With each goofy bite, confusion would reign,
Yet seeking delight was worth any pain.

A detour took me through a dragon's breath,
Where a fortune teller laughed out of death.
She said, 'In chaos, you'll find gold',
But all I found was a sock left cold.

So here I am, with life as my muse,
Following twists, making whimsical hues.
With unseen paths and directions absurd,
I learn that laughter is truly preferred.

A Pilgrim's Journey Through the Unknown

Packed my bag with hopes and fears,
Left behind my comforting sneers.
With every step, a tumble and twist,
I discovered the joy in being missed.

Met a raccoon who offered a snack,
Said, 'Forget the map; follow your knack.'
Danced with raindrops, sang to the breeze,
I found meaning beneath the tall trees.

Chased a cloud that looked like a duck,
Laughed at the mud, said, 'What the...!'
Turns out the path isn't meant to be straight,
Life's more fun at the hands of fate.

So here I roam, a pilgrim with glee,
Grateful for every misplaced decree.
With humor my compass, I'll wander and play,
In this grand adventure, I find my way.

Uncharted Territories of the Heart

In a forest of feelings, I took a wrong turn,
Found a squirrel who taught me how to discern.
Lost in a maze of thoughts, hey, what a surprise!
A raccoon gave me fashion tips—what a prize!

Twisted paths and crumbs of fate,
I was searching for love, or maybe just cake.
The sun set on my quest, a typical caper,
But I ended up with a fluffy green paper!

Adventures abound in this strange little chase,
Got tangled in laughter, a most awkward place.
With every misstep, I just couldn't complain,
For joy found its way through heartache and rain.

So here's to the winding, the weird, and the strange,
To finding your joy in a world full of change.
Each wrong turn, a giggle, a lesson so bright,
Navigating feelings, I'm lost—what a sight!

Finding Stars in the Dark

In twilight's embrace, the stars play peek-a-boo,
I misread my map, but what's a girl to do?
Chasing sparkles, I stumbled on air,
Tripped over wishes, oh, life's not so rare!

A comet whipped by, said, 'Follow the fun!'
Each twinkle a promise, each giggle a pun.
When darkness descends, just dance with the night,
For who needs a plan when you've got pure delight?

I found constellations in the depths of my head,
They whispered sweet nothings as I lay in bed.
Lost in my thoughts, I was finally found,
In laughter-filled moments where joy knows no bound.

So grab a sparkler, and let's light up the sky,
With mischief and magic that soar ever high.
In the chaos of wandering, a treasure awaits,
Finding stars in the dark helps the heart celebrate!

Fragments of a Fractured Compass

With a compass that spins like a disco ball,
I set off to find where I'd stashed my all.
Each point battled hard, while I begged for a guide,
But my GPS was down—let the antics abide!

I traveled through puddles that looked like the sea,
Met a frog with opinions and a predilection for tea.
He croaked out my fortune, said, 'Try door number three!'

Guess which door opened? Just a nap and a spree!

Wandered in circles, my thoughts doing flips,
Conversations with shadows—oh, how time slips!
Clutching at breadcrumbs, my map made of dreams,
Each detour a venture, or so it still seems.

So here's to the fragments where whacky meets wise,
In the midst of confusion, joy always will rise.
With every wrong turn in this grand merry dance,
I find new adventures — come join the romance!

The Dance of the Wayfarer

With two left feet, I tango through life,
Each twirl a mishap, oh, the delightful strife.
I'll skirt past the troubles with a grin ear to ear,
For the clumsy can waltz when there's laughter near!

The wind plays the drums, and I'm lost in the sound,
Swaying with squirrels on this whimsical ground.
A spin here, a slide there, oh, what a delight,
I discover the joy of each misstep at night!

Under the stars, with a partner—my fears,
I'm prancing and laughing, sprouting new cheers.
Life's unpredictable, but so is the beat,
Just follow the rhythm with your own silly feet!

So raise a glass high to the moments we stray,
For the dance of the wayfarer brightens the day.
In getting a bit lost, we find treasures so rare,
The tune calls us onward, let's dance without care!

A Symphony of Wayward Beats

In the maze of socks, I trip and tumble,
Chasing thoughts like cats, I often stumble.
The maps all sing a tune, quite absurd,
And I'm the maestro, conducting a herd.

Through puddles of doubt, I skip and hop,
My compass points nowhere, but I can't stop.
I dance with the trees, in a waltz of grace,
Seeking treasure based on a squirrel's face.

The stars hold secrets, like a cheeky jest,
I ask for directions; they send me west.
But hey! That's the charm of roads less taken,
With giggles like confetti, I laugh at the shaken.

So here's to the lost, and the nearly found,
In upside-down worlds, where fun abounds.
Let's toast to the twisty paths we roam,
Each detour a melody, leading us home.

Navigating the Unknown

With a map drawn by a toddler, I set off one day,
In search of adventure, in a most curious way.
The signs twist and turn, like my wayward thoughts,
As I dodge all the tangles that life often plots.

I ask for a route, but folks just laugh loud,
I'm the punchline, it's clear, in this whimsical crowd.
A dog leads the way with a bouncing delight,
And I'm left to ponder, "Is this all just a sight?"

Through fields of lost buttons and runaway keys,
I trip over puddles and laugh with the breeze.
Each turn is a riddle, a raucous surprise,
With everything silly, and laughter that flies.

In this dance with the lost, I learn to be free,
With giggles as guides, how silly can we be?
My heart finds the rhythm, through wrongs and rights,
In the game called "Find Me," the joy ignites.

Whispers from the Abyss

In the depths of lost thoughts, the echoes do cackle,
Like a chicken in boots, oh what a debacle!
I wander through mazes of ice cream and cake,
While pondering deeply on choices I make.

There's a sock on the ceiling, all lonely and sad,
I swear it's a sign from my laundry, how mad!
With each little giggle, I dance on the floor,
The abyss brings me whispers, I just can't ignore.

The things that I ponder, absurd yet profound,
Make me question the wisdom that's floating around.
Banana peels slip, oh how I do giggle,
In this carnival of chaos, I start to wiggle.

With spirits a-laughing, I'll wander this path,
Finding meaning in mishaps and bursts of pure wrath.
For whispers are secrets from the great wide blue,
And sometimes losing is simply the new.

The Serpent's Embrace

In gardens of nonsense, a serpent I greet,
It coils and it wiggles, with charm and some heat.
I ask for its wisdom, "Oh serpent so sly,
What truth do you weave as we dance in the sky?"

With a wink and a hiss, it tells me to chill,
"To laugh at confusion, embrace every thrill.
For I twist and I turn, a rhythm of fate,
And finding your path is to dance, not to wait."

So off I do go, skipping stones on the stream,
With giggles in pockets and wild, crazy dreams.
The serpent just smiles, its laughter like silk,
In this waltz of the foolish, I find my own milk.

From snafus to giggles, my journey unfolds,
With each turn, each stumble, and adventures untold.
So here's to the serpent and tangled, mad fates,
To get lost is a blessing, let's open the gates!

The Lament of the Wayward Traveler

I packed my bags with snacks and dreams,
But I forgot my map, or so it seems.
I turned left when I should have gone right,
Now I'm dancing with squirrels in the moonlight.

My GPS insists I'm near a lake,
But I see a pond with a big ol' snake.
I asked a goose for some directions,
It just quacked back, full of deflections.

I drank some coffee at the wrong café,
The barista laughed, said, "Have a nice day!"
I spilled my brew all over my lap,
And now I'm wearing a soggy mishap.

Yet in this chaos, I start to grin,
Every wrong turn feels like a win.
With every mishap, I learn to flow,
Guess that's just how the wild winds blow!

Unraveled Threads of Existence

I knitted a sweater for my pet cat,
But somehow, I ended up with a hat.
The yarn got tangled in quite the mess,
Now he looks like a fashion-obsessed princess!

I thought I'd weave a grand tapestry,
But I've made a sack intended for me.
It's filled with dreams and crumbs from lunch,
I guess my tapestry is more of a bunch!

Each thread I pull comes undone with glee,
Like my attempts at a simple cup of tea.
The kettle whistled a melodious tune,
While I danced 'round the kitchen like a cartoon!

Embracing the chaos, I've found my charm,
In every mishap, I'll raise the alarm.
Unraveled lines still make a great art,
Guess that's the trick—just follow your heart!

Where the Heart Finds Its Echo

I wandered into a forest so green,
Thought I'd find peace, but it felt like a dream.
Found a frog who claimed he was the king,
He croaked advice that made my heart sing!

I stumbled upon a stream bubbly and bright,
Where fish wore glasses and played every night.
They told me my worries were just in my head,
So I joined their dance, completely misled!

In this place, I twirled like a fool on the run,
Chasing my shadow, just having some fun.
The echoes of laughter rang loud in the air,
With every hop, I shed all my care.

I may never find my intended goal,
But in wild mischief, I found my soul.
In the heart of the forest, I've come to see,
Sometimes losing your way is just being free!

Whirlwinds of Uncertainty

I set sail on a ship made of dreams,
Thinking I'd conquer the mighty streams.
But the winds had plans, blew me off course,
Now I'm stranded on the shore of remorse!

I tried my hand at catching the breeze,
Instead, I caught seaweed—oh, what a tease!
The dolphins laughed as I twirled in the foam,
Claiming aquatic antics would lead me home.

I took a plunge into the swirling sea,
But forgot to come up—just a fish, oh me!
Now I'm practicing my flippered dance,
Turns out ocean flow is quite a romance!

Through whirlwinds of doubt, I learned to be bold,
In the lively chaos, I've found my gold.
For in every tumble, every swirl and twist,
A splash of surprise cannot be missed!

The Journey of Forgotten Roads

In a world where paths twist and turn,
I tripped on a stone, and I took a wrong burn.
With a map upside-down, I'm lost in the breeze,
Chasing my tail like a dog chasing fleas.

I found a café with bread made of cheese,
The barista just laughed, said, "Whatever you please!"
So I sipped on my drink, all fizzy and bright,
And searched for directions in the glow of the light.

The locals all smirked, they knew I was lost,
"Just follow your nose, it won't matter the cost."
So I head to the left, then I dart to the right,
Hoping to stumble upon a clear sight.

With each silly turn, new friends come alive,
In the mix of the chaos, together we thrive.
So here's to the blunders, the laughs, and the cheer,
For getting all lost is what brought me right here.

Serendipity in the Mist

I woke up one morning, all foggy and gray,
Thought I'd stroll my dog, give my worries away.
But the mist had me puzzled, confusion my friend,
My dog took a lead, where he thought we should end.

I stopped at a corner and met a lost cat,
Who sat like a guru on a fuzzy straw hat.
"Did you lose your way?" she purred with a grin,
"Or are you just seeking the chaos within?"

Next came a turtle, so slow, oh so grand,
He told me, "Dear friend, take it easy, just stand.
Sometimes the joy's in the paths that we take,
You'll find all you seek in the pie that you bake!"

So I squinted through fog, found a bakery shop,
With donuts and muffins, oh boy, what a stop!
For in twists and in turns, through the mist, I did roam,
In the hazy confusion, I found my way home.

When Stars Align in Solitude

Under a sky where the stars like to dance,
I sat by myself, missed my chance for romance.
A shooting star passed and it gave me a wink,
"Go make a new friend, don't just sit here and think!"

I chuckled at cosmos, how fickle their game,
When the universe giggles and I feel a bit lame.
So I gathered my courage, stood up from my seat,
And tripped on my shoelace, oh what a sweet feat!

A fairy in sneakers flew right past my nose,
With glittery wisdom, she whispered, "Who knows?
Sometimes when we wander away from our plans,
We stumble on laughter, or meet silly fans!"

As the moon twinkled bright, it shrugged off my strife,
Turns out being solo can spark genuine life.
In the dance of the stars, I found my birthright,
To laugh with the world, and feel utterly light.

Labyrinths of the Soul

In a maze made of mirrors, I wander my mind,
With thoughts wrapped in ribbons, so tangled and blind.
Each corner I turn, there's a chuckle or cheer,
A ghost in a tutu says, "Stop living in fear!"

I met a wise panda who taught me to bake,
He rolled up his sleeves, said, "Come on for your sake!"
With flour on faces, we crafted some fun,
He whispered, "Sweetie, it's okay to be spun!"

Lost in my antics, I stumbled on joy,
With a punchline for life, and a wild, quirky ploy.
The exits seemed further, yet laughter drew near,
While echoes of giggles stuffed worries with cheer.

Now I dance through the twists, not afraid of the fall,
In the puzzle of being, I've answered the call.
For amidst all the chaos and roles that we play,
There's humor in wandering, brightening my way.

Serendipity's Silent Dance

In a grocery store, I took a wrong turn,
Chasing a snack, oh how the tables would churn.
Found a lost cat, gave it my last donut,
Now I'm its owner, who's in the wrong rut!

I tried to map out a path that was clear,
But ended up lost on a back road of beer.
Met a guy named Chuck, he sold me a dream,
Turns out he just wanted to join my ice cream team!

Wandering through life like a bee on the run,
Buzzing through choices, searching for fun.
I tripped on my thoughts, landed in glee,
Just me, my ice cream, and cat on a spree!

So if you're feeling stuck, take a chance with a twirl,
Buy a snack or two, watch your worries unfurl.
For in the madness, sweet moments take flight,
Dancing through chaos, find your own light!

Fragments of a Wayward Soul

I wandered the streets with mismatched shoes,
Thought I'd find wisdom, but just found some blues.
A squirrel stole my burger, I gave it a glare,
It chattered in triumph, I flipped my last hair!

With GPS set, my route went awry,
Took a wrong turn, tried to reason why.
Found a café promising the best sweet treat,
Got a side of confusion with a laugh on my seat!

Met a guy with a compass that spun like a top,
Claimed he was searching for the best ice cream shop.
But we ended up at a bank, counting our coins,
Guess our adventure was hiding in odd joints!

So here's to the fragments, the detours, the blurs,
Life's a jumbled puzzle, not just neat little cures.
Laugh at the missteps, let joy be the goal,
In every mix-up, find the vibrant soul!

The Tapestry of Uncharted Paths

Stumbled on highways leading me astray,
Wore a hat of confusion on an unplanned day.
But oh, the surprises, like candy in jars,
Each twist a delight, with giggles and cars!

A parrot stole my sandwich, squawked with delight,
I waved it goodbye; it took off on its flight.
A mime turned my frown into a true work of art,
We danced in the street, I felt a new start!

Navigating this maze, with snacks in my pack,
Lost was the route, but joy was the track.
Met some folks selling what they called "good vibes,"
We bartered with laughter, and they won the bribes!

So weave your own tale, with threads bright and bold,
Through tangled adventures, find treasures untold.
For every misstep, a spark to ignite,
In the tapestry of wander, future shines bright!

Beneath the Stars of Lost Directions

Got lost in the woods looking for my shoe,
Ended up at a feast meant for a zoo!
With raccoons on tables and owls in the trees,
I joined their party, and we danced with the breeze!

Rode my bike, thinking I'd find some peace,
Ended up at a circus; oh, what a release!
The clowns were a riot, juggling my fears,
I laughed so hard, it brought joyful tears.

Tried to read maps, but they spoke in a code,
My compass went crazy; it spun and then strode.
Found a signpost pointing to "Free Ice Cream,"
Chased after the taste, living my sweet dream!

Beneath a sky filled with stars oh-so-bright,
I learned that getting lost can feel just right.
In the chaos and whimsy, true meaning unfolds,
With laughter and ice cream, life's joys turn to gold!

The Melody of the Unexplored

In the forest of my thoughts,
I tripped over a squirrel's tale.
It giggled at my lost ideas,
And danced away without a fail.

Wandering beneath the stars,
I mistook a bush for a friend.
It whispered secrets of the cosmos,
Then left me with a broken blend.

A GPS that goes haywire,
Sent me to a donut shop.
I pondered life's great mysteries,
While munching on a sugary top.

In this labyrinth of the absurd,
I found joy in twists and bends.
So here's to the tangled pathways,
Where laughter and adventure blends.

Unlocking the Hidden Maps

With a compass that points to nowhere,
I scribble on a napkin map.
Ignoring signs that say 'Not here',
I chase the future with a gap.

A treasure hunt for shiny dreams,
Yelled the parrot from the tree.
I followed it through sticky streams,
Only to find it lost with me.

Every twist reveals a giggle,
Or a frog that sings off key.
I stumble through a dance so fickle,
Where meaning's found in a cup of tea.

Unlocking every silly riddle,
With keys I've lost, then found anew.
My heart a map of playful dribble,
Leading me to joy, not rue.

Treading the Undefined

On invisible paths I stagger,
Like a cat on roller skates.
Each step's a laugh, a silly swagger,
Navigating through the fates.

With mismatched socks and tangled hair,
I wade through puddles in my mind.
A compass broken beyond repair,
Yet fun is what I hope to find.

The road ahead looks quite confusing,
Like a jigsaw with no start.
But each stumble feels more amusing,
As laughter blooms inside my heart.

So I'll tread on, a quiet cheer,
For every wrong turn sparks delight.
Even when the end's unclear,
The dance of joy feels ever right.

Reflections on the Nature of Search

In mirrors cracked and frames askew,
  I seek reflections that betray.
What's true might spark a snicker too,
  As shadows play in bright array.

Searching for the meaning's song,
  In grocery aisles, I often roam.
The cereal boxes sing along,
They fill my cart, my heart, my home.

I ask the wise as I stroll by,
The cat grinned with a knowing purr.
I chuckled soft—I asked it why,
  It said, "Why not? Just be a blur!"

So here I wander, laughs abound,
  In every quest, a quirky twist.
Finding joy in what I've found,
And missed the things I thought I wished.

A Kaleidoscope of Wayward Moments

In a world where maps are just for show,
I wandered off with a cheer and a glow.
Found myself in a land made of pie,
Where squirrels debated and unicorns fly.

I asked a rabbit for directions, you see,
He pointed to a tree with a sign that said 'Free!'.
But the tree was just laughing, a true prankster's delight,
I danced with the shadows under the moonlight.

In my quest to decipher the clouds overhead,
I tripped on a rainbow, but that's how I tread!
With sparkles and giggles, I still lose my way,
Finding gems in the chaos, come what may.

So here's to the moments that twist and they veer,
To the joy in the jumbles and laughter, let's cheer!
For every wrong turn leads to a grin,
In this kaleidoscope, let the fun begin!

The Daring Quest for Inner Wholeness

Off I went on a daring escapade,
Searching for answers in a cosmic parade.
Got distracted by donuts at the first stoplight,
A sweet diversion, oh what a sight!

A wise old owl hooted, perched on my fries,
Said, 'Inner peace comes with extra size!'
So I munched on that wisdom, a crunchy delight,
While pondering planets that danced in the night.

Came across a dog wearing spectacles grand,
He told me to wander upon shifting sand.
Chasing my dreams was a wild, wriggly race,
Until I tripped over my own shoelace.

Yet strides I did take, in a zigzaggy flight,
Trading confusion for giggles and light.
In the chaos, I found my wobbly spine,
In flavors and fur, I learned to define!

Moments Adrift in Time

Time traveled swiftly on a butterfly's wing,
Drifting through puddles where daydreams sing.
Met a clock that was stuck and could only say 'Maybe',
While I danced with a fish that was feeling quite lazy.

In the back of my mind, thoughts spun like a top,
Making sense of nonsense, it wouldn't stop.
I found space for silliness in every dull tick,
Juggling my worries, oh, wasn't it slick?

Each hour a riddle, each minute a joke,
The tick-tock band played while I tried to poke.
At the heart of the baffled, I stumbled on gold,
In moments adrift, the real stories unfold.

So here I stand, with giggles in tow,
In the grand scheme of things, what do we know?
Time's but a riddle, like life is a game,
And in every misstep, we find laughter's flame!

The Mosaic of Uncertainty

In a world painted bright with splashes of doubt,
I scurried around, but what was it about?
The puzzle was missing a piece here and there,
Yet I laughed off the chaos, as if I had flair.

A jigsaw of whimsy, I danced in between,
With colors of fortune and mischief unseen.
At a corner café, bold choices I made,
Bravely drinking coffee with a splash of grenade!

Each twist in the road had a bounce to its beat,
Had me tap dancing with squirrels on the street.
Found wisdom in giggles, a hearty surprise,
Uncertainty sharpened my curious eyes.

So here's to the whimsical, the messy and wild,
To embracing our quirks just like a child.
In this mosaic we craft, let's relish the chance,
To revel in chaos, and join in the dance!

The Phoenix of Lost Journeys

I flew too high, then hit the ground,
Like that bird with a flair, who never found.
My map was upside down, the stars off track,
But hey, at least I got a snack!

Detours led me to a giant pie,
With whipped cream that could make a grown man cry.
In every tumble, a new surprise,
A joke from fate, right before my eyes.

Each stumble taught me how to dance,
In clumsy twirls and silly prance.
I wear my scars like a badge of cheer,
For what's a journey without some jeer?

So here I stand, not quite a sage,
With stories that could fill a page.
I chase the sun, not knowing where,
And laugh at life's wild, crazy fare.

Embracing the Shadows Within

In a closet dark, I took a peek,
Found old shoes and a rubber beak.
Waded through memories, a little absurd,
Like a cat trying to fly, it's just unheard.

I whispered secrets to my ghost,
Who grinned and said, "I love a roast!"
Together we danced, a spooky jig,
In the quiet moments, all feelings big.

I tripped on my thoughts, fell on a cat,
She laughed, then scratched me, imagine that!
Embracing shadows, we took a leap,
Into funny stories that made me weep.

From darkness blooms a wild delight,
Like cake at midnight, quite a sight.
So here's to chaos, fun, and grin,
Embrace those shadows—let the laughter begin!

Wandering Through Shadows

With my sights set high, I lost my way,
Stumbled on a joke in the broad light of day.
Every twist and turn, a laugh to find,
A penguin in shorts? Well, that's just kind!

I followed the moon, or so I thought,
Ended up with crabs—who would've fought?
In a sea of misfits, I found my crew,
A talking fish and a parrot, too!

We shared some tales over fizzy drinks,
Of how life's a puzzle, so full of kinks.
With every laugh, confusion fades,
In the whirl of the fun, where joy cascades.

Through winding paths, with giggles abound,
I found my heart in the silliest sound.
So let's frolic in shadows, make mischief our crown,
For in playful wandering, true joy is found.

The Compass Within

I bought a compass that spun with flair,
Pointed to dinner instead of where!
With directions all mixed up, I did a twirl,
Found ice cream instead—oh, what a whirl!

Every wrong turn felt like a dance,
When you give chaos a chance to prance.
I chased my tail in the streetlight glow,
Where laughter echoed, just like a show.

In endless circles, I made a friend,
Who also had no clue where they'd end.
Together we wandered, aimless and bright,
Turning missteps into starlit flight.

So here's my compass, it points to fun,
Through giggles and chaos, we run, run, run.
With every detour, my heart's on a spree,
For what's lost in wander is really just me!

The Intersection of Stray Thoughts

I took a turn left instead of a right,
My GPS protested, lost all its might.
Chasing clouds with a grin and a wink,
Maybe missteps help us think!

A squirrel waved as I sailed on by,
Was he judging me, that beady-eyed guy?
Or just wondering where I call home,
In my car I feel like a rolling poem.

Road signs flirt with directions bizarre,
Each twist and turn, a chance to go far.
I stop for coffee, lost track of time,
And laugh at my map, which doesn't rhyme.

Who knew chaos could be such good fun?
A stumble today could mean a pun won.
With every wrong path, I gain a new view,
Maybe getting lost is the best thing to do!

Embracing the Chaotic Map

With a map full of doodles, I set out to roam,
Each line is a giggle, a thread of a poem.
Directions? Ha! I'd rather just guess,
Finding treasure in each silly mess.

A roundabout brought me to a petting zoo,
Where goats gave me looks that said, 'Who are you?'
I followed a cat, what wisdom I sought,
But ended up dancing with a chicken I caught.

Every detour's a chance to delight,
Like tripping on nothing in broad daylight.
Mismatched socks and food bits on my shirt,
Who knew chaos could spare me the hurt?

So here's to the roads that lead us a stray,
To the wacky and wild that color our day.
With each unexpected laugh, grasp, and tussle,
I let out a chuckle and gather my bustle!

Scattered Shards of Meaning

A puzzle of thoughts all jumbled and cracked,
I searched for the edges, but they stayed abstract.
With each mismatched piece, I giggled and frowned,
Wondering what wisdom in messes I've found.

I tripped on my laces, fell straight in a bush,
Amidst the soft leaves, I felt quite the rush.
A squirrel cackled, he seemed to agree,
That sometimes the branches are better than trees.

A paper airplane flew by with a laugh,
It twisted and turned like a wild photograph.
Where's the destination? Who really knows?
We might find a party in life's little throes.

So here's to the scraps that line our way,
The quirky reflections that brighten the gray.
Every shard found obscured in the rush,
May just be the crackle—the fun, the hush!

The Pulse of Vagabond Dreams

With a backpack of hopes and a compass that spins,
I chase down each whim, let the adventure begin.
The road ahead winks, it beckons and sways,
In a twisty old tango that dances and plays.

I pilot my ship on a soda can sea,
Where ceiling fan clouds drift endlessly.
A pirate on Mondays, a mermaid by noon,
Every detour a quest, my heart is in tune.

Laughter's the anchor that keeps me afloat,
While rubber fish guide me, they wiggle and gloat.
With each silly jaunt, I find treasure anew,
A heartbeat of chaos in skies painted blue.

So let's ride the waves of our whimsical schemes,
With mischief and giggles fueling our dreams.
For in every lost moment, a sparkle will gleam,
It's a feast of the splendid, the wild, the supreme!

The Art of Wayfinding

I wandered down a path unsure,
With signposts pointing to a cure.
But every turn felt like a trick,
I found a cat, which made me stick.

I asked a squirrel for advice,
He chattered loudly, wasn't nice.
"Just keep on going, you'll be fine!"
I wondered if he drank some wine.

A crowd of ducks became my guide,
They quacked, and I could not abide.
With webbed feet they held a parade,
We made it halfway, then they swayed.

The exit sign, a distant dream,
I turned around, life's comedy team.
With laughter echoing through the maze,
I realized fun was the better phase.

Labyrinths of the Mind's Eye

In a maze of memories, I roam,
I thought I had arrived back home.
But the fridge was all empty, oh no!
I guess I'm lost in my own show.

A jigsaw puzzle with pieces stray,
I try to fit them in a way.
The picture's blurred – is that a cat?
Perhaps it's time for a chitchat!

My thoughts do salsa, cha-cha too,
They spin around like a dizzy crew.
I asked my shoes for some insight,
They just squeaked back, "It's a wild night!"

Frantically searching through the haze,
I find humor in this mental maze.
With giggles echoing through my head,
I'll laugh my way home instead.

Searching for the Unwritten Map

I pulled out my map, full of scribbles,
Marked with coffee stains and dribbles.
Each line was wobbly, dashed about,
Yet adventure came with every route.

I asked a frog, "Where's the nearest road?"
He croaked and jumped, then off he strode.
I followed suit, but slipped in a puddle,
I might be lost, but never in a muddle!

With breadcrumbs left as trail markers true,
I found a flock of sheep to pursue.
"Bahh-lieve in yourself!" they all bleated,
Their wisdom, it seemed, was unseated!

Through wacky twists and turns I went,
Each misstep was a new lament.
Yet laughter bloomed where fear had festered,
In this wild search, my heart had festered.

Footprints on a Foggy Dawn

In the misty morning, I stroll with style,
My slippers squish with each wobbly mile.
The world is hazy, my head's quite spun,
I fumble a bit, but it's all in good fun.

I spot some footprints, a curious trail,
Could it be deer? Or maybe a snail?
I followed them down to a muddy pit,
Where a turtle sat, and he wouldn't quit.

"Where are we going?" I asked in glee,
He just blinked slow; he's wise, you see.
"Patience, young grasshopper, take your time,
Adventures unfold; it's honestly sublime!"

As the fog lifts, I giggle in glee,
Since all paths lead to quirky jubilee.
Through laughter and blunders, I stride with ease,
Finding joy in the moments and sweet little pleas.

Whispers in the Maze

In a tangle of streets, I spun around,
My map upside down, lost without sound.
The squirrels chuckled, they must know the way,
As I dodged all the pigeons that boldly held sway.

With each winding turn, I tripped on my feet,
A dog eyed me close, oh what a treat!
"Follow your nose!" it seemed to bark out,
But my sense of direction was all but in doubt.

A signpost appeared, its arrow so sly,
"To the nearest café," it made me comply.
But I'm still not sure if I'm lost or just free,
Sipping a latte while the world laughs at me.

So here I'll stay, in this cozy café,
With laughter and pastries to brighten my day.
Who knew getting lost could feel so divine?
I'll take another slice of that sweet lemon line!

Echoes of the Wandering Heart

My heart took a stroll, with no map in hand,
It danced through the wild, across glittering sand.
Each step was a giggle, a hop and a skip,
With echoes of mischief, I'd flip and I'd trip.

I met a strange man with shoes of pure glee,
Who claimed he could show me what it means to be free.
He led me in circles, round and round we went,
Until we both stopped, our laughter unbent.

A bird joined in, perched on my shoulder,
"Just trust in the chaos, and you'll grow bolder!"
With a wink and a flap, it took off in a whirl,
I marveled at the clouds, spun up like a girl.

So here's to the journeys that lead us astray,
Where laughter's the compass, and whims are the way.
In echoes of joy, we find our true part,
Wandering freely with each wandering heart.

The Compass of Forgotten Dreams

Once I had a compass, it pointed success,
But it ran off one day, causing me such stress.
The dreams I had tucked, like socks that went rogue,
Played tag in the clouds, like a friendly old frog.

I stumbled upon a map with no chart,
It led me to places with a strangely warm heart.
A tree offered lemonade, and kittens in hats,
While dancing and twirling like acrobatic cats.

I followed the laughter, and lo and behold,
Forgotten dreams shimmered, all daring and bold.
They winked as they whispered, "You've got it all wrong,

Success isn't a straight line, it's a silly old song."

So here with my compass, I'm lost, and it's fine,
For joy is a treasure, and I've found my own shine.
I'll keep strumming tunes, with laughter my theme,
In the compass of days filled with whimsical dreams.

Shadows in the Crossroads

At dusk, I arrived at a fork in my path,
With shadows that giggled, invoking a laugh.
One way looked scary, a haunted old route,
The other wore glitter, all sparkly and cute.

"So which way to go?" I pondered aloud,
At least not a monster, just shadows, not crowd.
Like a riddle they whispered, "It all depends,
On where you are headed, and how this one ends."

With a shrug and a smile, I flipped a soft coin,
It landed on laughter—hey, I think I'll join!
The shadows erupted, they danced around me,
In a party of quirks, so wild and so free.

As I twirled with those shadows, I found my own light,
In the mix of confusion, I felt so right.
With each wild decision, still chasing the gleam,
At crossroads of shadows, I followed my dream.

Light in the Labyrinth

In a maze of socks and shoes,
I search for paths to escape the blues.
A dust bunny leads with a wink,
Does this mean I need a drink?

Twists and turns in every hall,
I trip and laugh, I almost fall.
A map in hand, but it's a joke,
Who knew the cat was the real bloke?

Found my way to the laundry room,
Where missing shirts begin to bloom.
I hear the dryer sing a song,
Maybe here I truly belong!

So off I go, with glee and cheer,
Embracing all that seems unclear.
I'll dance on socks, a joyful spree,
For this lost soul, it's meant to be!

The Compass of Resilience

My compass spins, what a surprise!
North is south, oh how it lies!
It points to snacks, not to the shore,
Why worry when there's chips galore?

I wander forth on this strange quest,
With trail mix crumbs to be my fest.
I trip on dreams, but down I fall,
Yet laughter carries me through it all.

A squirrel mocks, it steals my nut,
As if to say, 'Why not be glut?'
Yet through the woods, I grin and toil,
For in the mess, my soul will boil.

So here I am, with snacks in hand,
Defining joy in this strange land.
With each misstep, I learn to sway,
Finding magic in the fray!

Discoveries Beneath the Surface

Under the bed, what do I find?
Old shoes, a toy, and maybe my mind.
Dust bunnies dance like they're in charge,
Making deep thoughts feel quite large.

I dive for treasures, a brave explorer,
Uncovering relics, oh, what a horror!
A sock with a hole, a half-eaten snack,
Guess this adventure is on the right track!

The cat oversees with utmost glee,
As I dig up forgotten history.
A T-Rex toy, a feathery hat,
Joking around with this treasure trove chat.

So here I sift through past's parade,
Making mischief, unafraid.
Beneath the surface, smiles abound,
In lost and found, true joy is found!

Wandering Towards Clarity

With my eyes half shut, I roam the hall,
Seeking the fridge, but tripping on my shawl.
Coffee's my goal, but the cat's in the way,
What's his obsession with making me sway?

Every step is a wobbly quest,
Exploring each corner, I'm truly blessed.
The dog joins in with a bark and a chase,
Suddenly, I'm in a slapstick race!

Through puddles of cereal and crumbs of bread,
The quest for clarity fills me with dread.
Yet laughter erupts like a sudden sneeze,
Finding joy in chaos, like a warm summer breeze.

So let me wander, let me roam free,
In this odd journey, with snacks and glee.
With every misstep, a smile now glows,
In this dance of chaos, my spirit flows!

www.ingramcontent.com/pod-product-compliance
Lightning Source LLC
Chambersburg PA
CBHW051631160426
43209CB00004B/604